Apples for Cheyenne

A story about autism, horses, and friendship.

Elizabeth King Gerlach
Illustrated by Kim Miller

Apples for Cheyenne

All marketing and publishing rights guaranteed to and reserved by:

FUTURE HORIZONS INC.

817-277-0727
817-277-2270 Fax

Web site: www.fhautism.com
E-mail: info@fhautism.com

ISBN: 978-1-935274-22-3

Dedication

To all the horses and riders who love them.

Cheyenne is a horse who lives in a big red barn near the sea.

On the drive there, Rachel smells the salty air.

She watches the waves from the corner of her eyes. It is Monday—time for a horseback ride!

Rachel can walk well, but she has autism.

People with autism have special needs. Their bodies and brains don't work in the same way as other people's. Rachel can use some words, but not as many as other kids her age.

Cheyenne doesn't mind. A horse does not need to hear words to be a friend.

4

Ben and Julie are already at the barn. They will have a riding lesson too.

Julie rides Pixie. Julie likes to move around a lot. It can be hard for her to sit still. She is already on her horse and ready to go!

Ben rides Coco. When he's not on a horse, Ben uses a wheelchair.

Their horses don't care. And it does not stop the children from riding.

The barn is full of strong smells. Some smells bother Rachel a lot, but she is used to these. She has been riding for three months.

The barn has eight stalls where the horses stay. Cheyenne's stall is the second one on the left. He stamps his foot. He is ready to go outside.

Rachel looks into Cheyenne's round, brown eyes.
His eyes have long, black lashes.

Rachel has trouble looking into other people's eyes,
but not into Cheyenne's. His eyes are gentle and do not
scare her. She can see herself in his eyes. They are like a
mirror.

Cheyenne looks in Rachel's eyes, too. He blinks at her
and sniffs at her coat pocket.

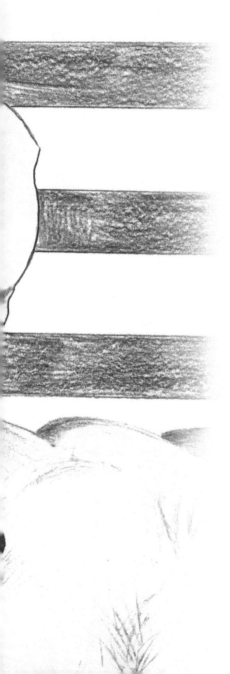

Cheyenne is patient while Rachel puts on her helmet.

"Hi, Chey," says Rachel. She pats him on the shoulder.

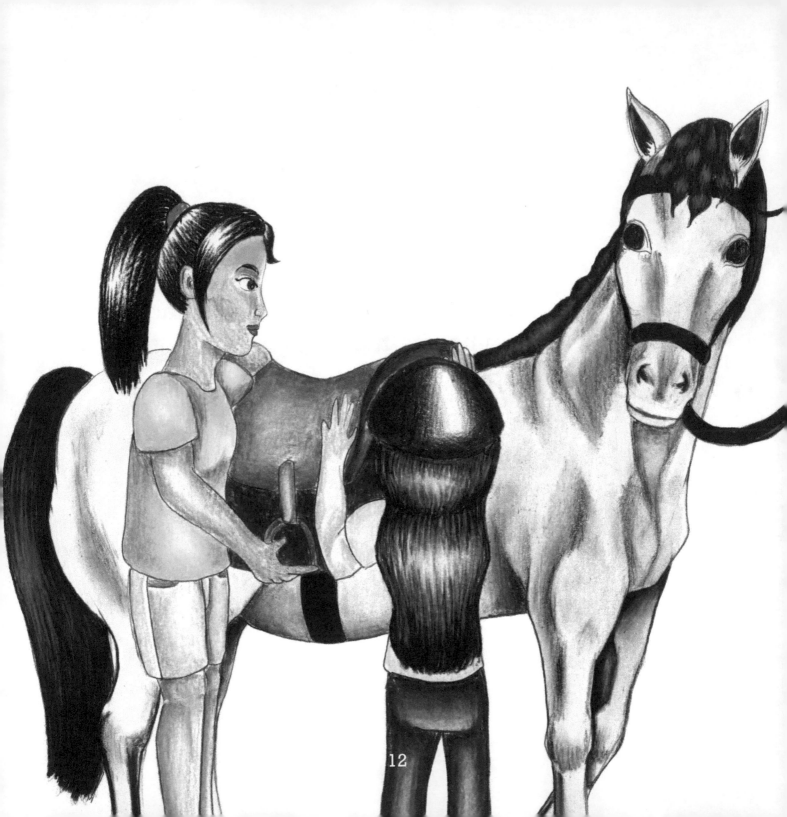

12

Rachel's teacher, Lana, helps her put on Cheyenne's saddle and bridle. Rachel takes the rainbow-colored reins and leads Cheyenne to the ramp. The ramp is outside the barn.

Ben rolls his wheelchair up the ramp and gets on Coco from there. Rachel likes to use the ramp because she can get on Cheyenne all by herself.

Lana leads Cheyenne and Coco out to the corral. Julie is waiting for them there. She fidgets in her saddle. She is ready to start riding!

16

They start by walking around the ring. This helps the horses and riders get to know each other after a whole week apart.

As she rides, Rachel can hear the ocean across the road. She hears better than most people. Some sounds hurt her ears, but not the ocean.

Rachel gives Cheyenne a little kick, and he begins to trot. Rachel smiles and laughs when Cheyenne trots. It feels good to her. Cheyenne likes to trot, too. He was born to do it.

Around and around the ring they go. Ben rides Coco next to Rachel. "Do you want to race?" asks Ben. Rachel doesn't answer Ben, but she gives Cheyenne another little kick. Off they go! Rachel passes Coco and Ben. But they aren't far behind.

Later, they go on a trail ride down to the sea. The grass in the pasture is tall and smells sweet. If Rachel is not careful, Cheyenne will try to eat the grass and forget to walk! Rachel loves to ride near the ocean.

She likes the steady sound of the waves. To her they always sound the same.

Julie and Pixie lead the way. Julie likes to focus her eyes right between the horse's ears. That steadies her.

Ben is behind them. Lana walks next to Cheyenne. Rachel likes to look back at the long line of hoof prints they leave in the sand.

24

Rachel hums as she rides. This is one of the ways she shows she is happy.

A seagull flies overhead. It squawks! Julie looks up and squawks back. Watching the seagull fly overhead makes Julie a little dizzy.

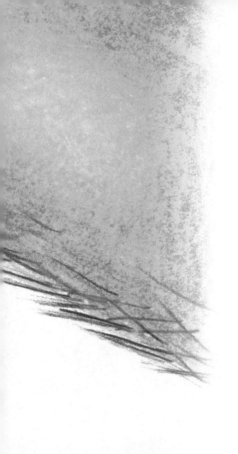

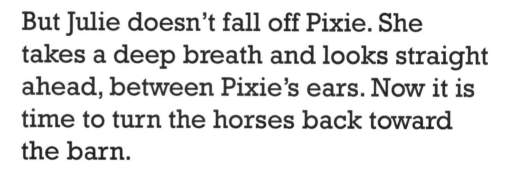But Julie doesn't fall off Pixie. She takes a deep breath and looks straight ahead, between Pixie's ears. Now it is time to turn the horses back toward the barn.

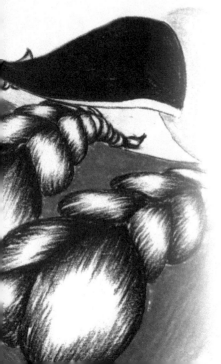

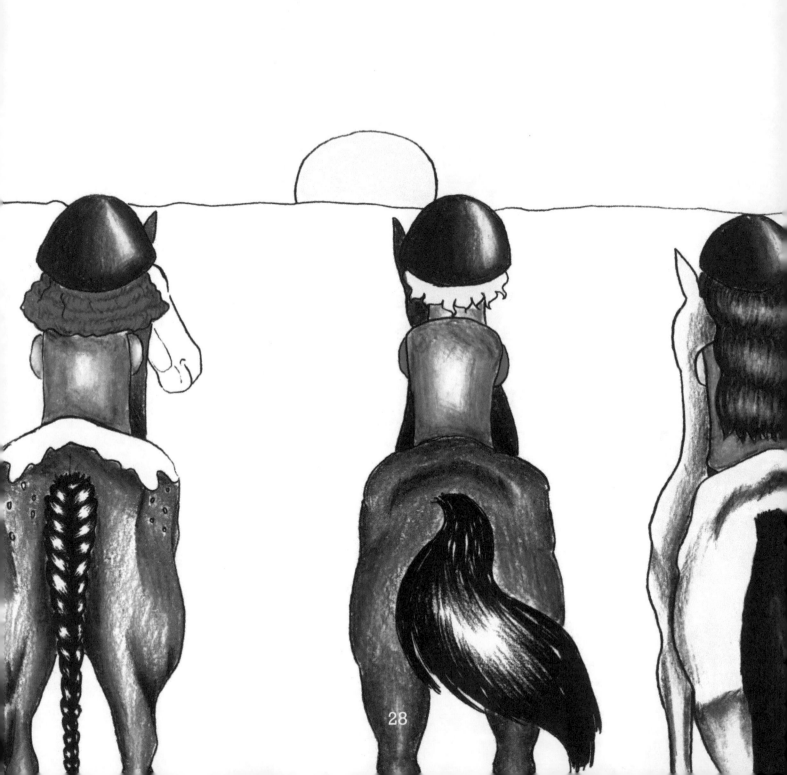

28

"Whoa," says Rachel. She knows this means stop. She pulls on the reins until Cheyenne slows down. Then Rachel pulls the reins to the right.

Cheyenne turns around. He flicks his tail and whinnies. Does he know something is waiting for him back at the barn?

The horses and riders go back to the big red barn. Rachel gets off Cheyenne and leads him into his stall. She helps Lana take off the saddle, then the blanket, then the bridle. She brushes Cheyenne's coat until it's smooth and shiny.

"Good job, Rachel," says Lana. Rachel hums and smiles.

Rachel's mother calls to her from the barn door. "It's time to give Cheyenne his treat!"

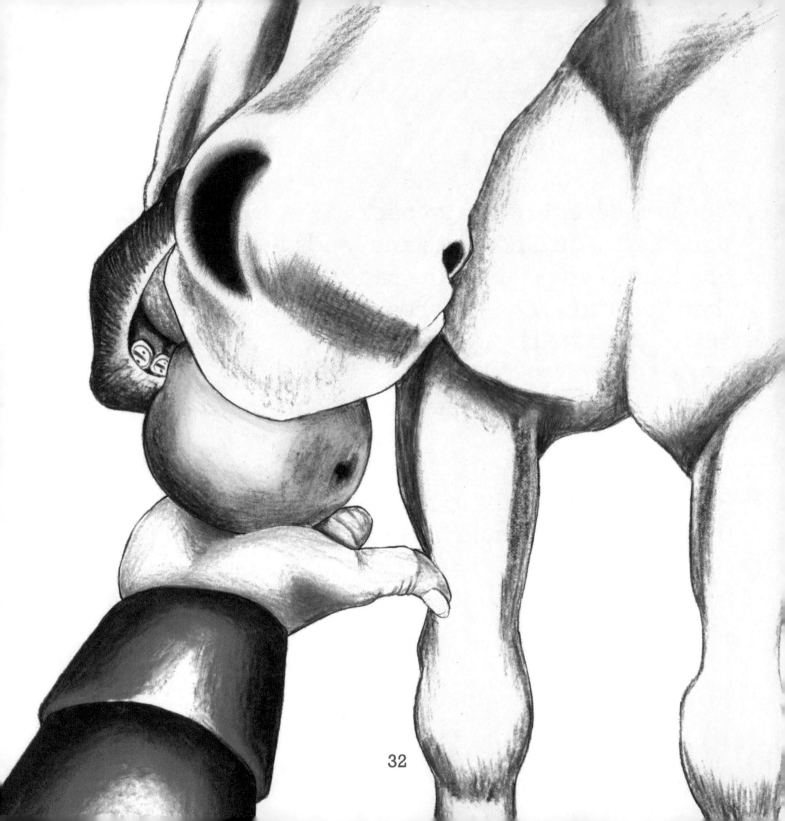

32

Rachel pulls an apple from her coat pocket. "Eat, Chey," she says to the horse.

She holds the apple with her hand flat, the way Lana taught her. Cheyenne sniffs the apple, then takes it from her hand. Munch! He loves to eat apples.

While Cheyenne eats his apple, Rachel rocks back and forth. Rocking feels good to her body, the way riding Cheyenne feels good. It helps her feel calm. She waits beside Cheyenne until he finishes eating the apple.

It is time to go.

"Bye, bye, Chey," Rachel says, as she strokes his cheek. The horse nuzzles her hand with his soft nose. His breath is warm. Rachel presses her cheek next to Cheyenne's.

36

Ben and Julie are already in their cars.
They all wave good-bye to each other.
Rachel and her mother get in their car.

38

On the drive home, Rachel stares out the car window at the waves of the sea.

Next Monday she will go for another horseback ride. She will bring another apple for Cheyenne.

Printed in the USA
CPSIA information can be obtained
at www.ICGtesting.com
JSHW072027140824
68134JS00042B/3815

9 781935 274223